The Wit and Wisdom of The Nanny™

The Wit and Wisdom of The Nanny™

Fran's Guide to Life, Love, and Shopping

Collected by Nan E. Fine

AVON BOOKS ◆ NEW YORK

THE WIT AND WISDOM OF "THE NANNY" is an original publication of Avon Books. This work has never before appeared in book form.

AVON BOOKS
A division of
The Hearst Corporation
1350 Avenue of the Americas
New York, New York 10019

Library of Congress Cataloging in Publication Data:

Fine, Nan E.
   The wit and wisdom of "The nanny" : Fran's guide to life, love, and shopping / Nan E. Fine.
      p.   cm.
1. American wit and humor.   I. Nanny (Television program).
II. Title.
PN6162.F475   1995   95-15089
791.45'72 — dc20   CIP

First Avon Books Trade Printing: November 1995

Quotes taken from episodic scripts written by:

Eve Ahlert & Dennis Drake, Alan R. Cohen & Alan Freedland, Fran Drescher & Peter Marc Jacobson, Pamela Eells & Sally Lapiduss, Alan Eisenstock & Larry Mintz, Lila Garrett, Andy Goodman, Janis Hirsch, Sandy Krinski, Bill Lawrence, Frank Lombardi, David M. Matthews, Lisa Medway, Howard Meyers, Howard Meyers & Diane Wilk, Tracy Newman & Jonathan Stark, Eileen O'Hare, Dana Reston, Dana Reston & Frank Lombardi, Michael Rowe, Robert Sternin & Prudence Fraser, and Diane Wilk.

The Nanny on Men

Men can't be rushed. They're like chicken. You cook them too fast, they get tough. Whereas you take your time, let them simmer awhile, they fall apart in your hands.

I've often said that men and women should be treated equally.
Except that men should still open doors and pick up the check.

At the grocery store, everything you need to know about a man is right there in his cart. If there's Midol, keep moving. Corn pads means he lives with his mother. I learned that the hard way. Also, two men with sweaters tied around their necks buying pesto, save yourself the pain.

As I told Mr. Sheffield, Maggie's got to learn how to handle herself with fourteen-year-old boys, so when she's grown up she'll know how to handle herself with men, who, when you come to think of it, are a lot like fourteen-year-old boys.

A kite is like a really cute guy.
You give him some slack and let him
fly free, then at the end of the day,
you yank his string and reel him back in.

Ma said she fell in love with Daddy's dimples. Thank God, I've never seen them. Plus he treated her like a lady. Every weekend he took her out to his favorite restaurant, and he never once let her carry her own tray. Not many men are that gallant.

Do I Know Kids or What?

Brighton was worried about being shorter than the other kids. I told him not to worry. Boys always shoot right up after their bar mitzvah. When that didn't work, I pointed out that history is filled with short leaders. Look at Napoleon—four-foot-two and we're still eating his pastry.

These kids are too much. Sometimes I ask myself, what do they expect? I mean, I have two hands, not wands. Not that they haven't performed magic in their day.

Gracie didn't want to go to her first slumber party. I couldn't understand why. You get to eat like a pig, make phony phone calls, and puke your guts up. As I told her, it's a very special time in a young girl's life.

When I took Gracie to the doctor,
I told her not to worry. After all,
doctors are our friends. They spend
their whole lives studying and training
just so they can help people. Okay,
help people and drive a Mercedes.

When I was a girl we couldn't afford a Lamb Chop doll, so Grandma Yetta used to put on her white curly wig and take out her teeth. Then Grandpa would put his hand up her blouse . . . You know, I think a good time was had by all.

I'm trying to expose the kids to other cultures. They order Chinese, they learn how Jewish people eat.

As I tell the kids — be grateful.
Your father had to walk ten miles
in the snow to get to *his* limo.

School, thank God for school. I need
those seven hours of personal time.
I mean, how can I continue to be
the bright, vivacious nanny everyone
knows and loves if I have to
spend all day with the kids?

Kids are like a brassiere.
They divide and separate.

The Nanny on Dating

I dated a mortician. He was a great guy who owned his own business. Not a lot of repeat customers but certainly recession proof. A girl's gotta do what a girl's gotta do. I have to admit I had my prejudices, but honey, once you wear black, you never go back.

Some personal ads are such a joke. "Single, white female." That could mean anyone from Janet Reno to Madonna. "Exotic good looks." I'm seeing a depilatory problem.

I've had to wean myself off lots of stuff. Cigarettes, caffeine, my ex-boyfriend Danny. That one was tough. Whenever anyone burped garlic, I got a craving.

I want a relationship. A real
relationship. Like Luke and Laura.

Your boyfriend doesn't understand you? Probably it's because you're like all the Fine women. We're just too damn subtle.

Danny bought me a g-string
for my birthday.
It was so inappropriate.
It's a good thing my mother's birthday
was two days later
or I'd still be stuck with it.

Danny told me that he had to go through a cheap, sleazy affair to appreciate me. I had to point out he was with her for six months. He said he had to be sure.

Feel the need for revenge? Do what I
did when Danny dumped me
for Heather Biblow. Buy some Nair,
add it to her Pert Plus,
and the next day she's on her way
to buy her first Eva Gabor wig.

The Nanny on Big Hair and Beauty

Big hair makes
your hips look smaller.

Why is it whenever someone special comes over, your hair never comes out big enough?

The secret to blush is less is more.
Unlike hair spray, where more is better.

I'm known for my style, except for that corn row phase I went through after I saw *Ten*.

My hair. The outer shell is hair spray. Inside, there's gel, mousse, volumizer, a whole infrastructure. The only difference between me and the Kingdome is Astroturf.

There was the time I was in a beauty pageant and Ellen Nagdaman spiked me with six-inch heels. So, I switched her hair spray with a can of Pam. Sure, she won, but she couldn't keep that crown on her head for nothing.

I do *not* color my hair.
I just add a layer
of dark highlights.

I used to be a model. Not clothes, feet.
All the Fines have fabulous feet.
In fact, I feel that my feet
still have so much to say.

The Nanny on Herself

I just can't tame this damn charisma.
Can I help it if I effervesce?

Worried about old age? Not me. Personally, I plan to be a platinum-blond prune in Miami, yanking up my tube top, doin' the cha-cha with my Cuban houseboy.

When the doctor told me he wanted to take my tonsils out, I told him that unless he was talking about dinner and dancing, they weren't interested.

Oh, I love the smell
of nail polish in the morning.

Don't underestimate the power of these adenoids. I had next-door neighbors move closer to the airport.

I am a nanny. Anything that the kids
tell me goes no further. I'm like a
priest. Well, not exactly like a priest
because priests are celibate.
And I'm . . . actually I could be a priest.
Nah, I couldn't go for that Nehru collar.
A scoop is good, a V, off the shoulder
. . . all good for me. But a Nehru . . .

Of course, I understand guilt.
My people invented it.
But we made up for it with
the Salk vaccine and Streisand.

The Nanny on
Shopping and Clothes

There's so much going on in the old neighborhood. Take shopping, for instance. There's Ronnie's Slack Shack on Union Turnpike. You know it? It's next to Vinnie's Jacket Racket, right by The Blouse House.

Lord & Taylor giveth
and Lord & Taylor can taketh away

I'm so proud of my work with Gracie. The other day we went shopping. She tried on every pair of shoes in the store and bought nothing. When she made the salesman cry, I knew she had a gift.

I have never considered dressing for comfort. If you do, the next thing you know you're on line at Pathmark in orthopedic shoes buying Nair.

If it ain't half off,
it ain't on sale.

Let me tell you, for a grandmother, pink tissues are an attractive wrist and brassiere-strap ornament.

I was thinking about the Pilgrims.
How'd they know what to pack?
I mean, you're going to a new world.
Is it hot ... cold ... rainy? There's no
brochures.... So they all wear the
same thing and what a mistake. Very
few people look good in a big hat,
a big collar, *and* a big buckle.

The Nanny on Vacations and Food

We used to spend every summer in Miami. It was off-season rates, so we got to stay twice as long. Plus the Fontainbleau had a fabulous Seafood Extravaganza—all you can eat. Smorgasbord tip: Go right to the shrimp and lobster. Don't fill up on the soup and cheese.

I've never been to Paris,
but I've been dying to go ever since
"The Facts of Life" girls went there.

I have traveled in some pretty exclusive
circles. I sat at the Captain's table
in a Carnival cruise. I passed
the A-1 to Kathie Lee.

We don't go fast in my family. We Fines like to linger and be a burden to others for as long as possible.

At our house we're big on vintage beverages. In our storage bin we've got a case of Tab from the Bay of Pigs.

Some people say yoga is a great way to keep your energy up. For me, it's a Snickers and a Diet Coke.

The Nanny on School

I played Hodel in my third grade production of *Fiddler*. The *Flushing Observer* said, "Fran Fine was a stand-out as Tevye's lost but heavily made-up daughter."

In school, I was the Queen of Arts and Crafts. Then one day I left my favorite brush in the shellac, and it hardened overnight. I just walked away and never looked back.

Now, the boys me and Val grew up with were bad. Take Lenny Brown. The kid had a smoker's cough in the fourth grade. Of course, now he's a big shot at R. J. Reynolds.

In high school, I played the Reverend Mother in *The Sound of Music*. I put a scoop neck in my nun's habit and those hills were alive.

Don't knock the Jewish holidays.
They get you out of more school
than mono.

GYM CLASS IN FIVE MINUTES

I figured out how to get gym class down to a grand total of five minutes instead of forty-five. First, you get dressed, taking your time ... you're not a fireman. That's ten minutes. Then you volunteer to get the equipment—which is heavy, so you pull something: It's a side-ache, a charley horse, or a hernia, depending on how much time you need. God, I was good. So we're down to nineteen minutes. Just enough time to look for your contact. You know how long it takes to find a contact that doesn't exist? Fourteen minutes ... which brings our total class time down to five minutes. Anybody can get through five minutes of gym.

The Nanny on Daddy

When I first saw Daddy's new toupee,
I thought it had like a Bobby
Goldsboro thing happening. I asked
him about it. He said the stylist told
him it was the "Jack Lord" look. I told
him he had it on backwards.

Why can't I find a guy like Daddy?
Deaf and on a pension.

Daddy has corns, so he cuts out the tops of his shoes. The powder-blue socks and Bermuda shorts complete the look.

Daddy's not much of a businessman.
He bought into one of those
big-and-tall-men franchises—in Tokyo.

The Nanny on
the Fine Men

For some crazy reason, the men
married to Fine women
all tend to drink.

Hammertoes—a cruel, crippling condition caused by shoving your feet into high heels that are too small. And if you don't think that's painful, ask my Uncle Harvey.

Cousin Irving the plumber—before him
it wasn't called Flushing.

I had an Uncle Aaron who manufactured
hernia trusses. All of a sudden,
everybody's got a hernia.
P.S., his friend Bernie put one on
backwards and it cut off his circulation.
Double amputation. And we're not
talking legs. Jacoby & Meyers put
him right in the commercial. He's the
one with the high voice.

My Uncle Harvey—when he sang "Somewhere Over the Rainbow," you'd swear Judy was in the room.

Jack is always trying to one-up my mother. We buy a Skylark, he buys an El Dorado. We move to Flushing, he moves to Florida. She never won. Oh yeah, except that one time. She got a mustache before he did.

Dead, my uncle was. Right there on the couch. But we didn't even notice until the seventh-inning stretch when he did not. Fortunately, my auntie had plastic slipcovers so they simply wrapped him up and took him away. Like a giant Ziploc.

Of course, when we landed on Ellis
Island, they changed our name,
so now we don't know
who the hell we are.

Ma's Best Advice

- *My mother always says, "Blood is thicker than water. And you can wipe them both off plastic slipcovers."*
- *With my mother, it was feed a cold, feed a fever, feed a migraine ... you could gain ten pounds from a paper cut.*
- *"Don't starve yourself for a man. That's what control tops are for."*
- *I remember Amy Semel's sweet sixteen at the bowling alley. I was dying to go, but my mother had this thing about wearing other people's shoes. She was scared I'd get polio. Or was it planter's warts? It was something with a* p.

*The Nanny on
the Fine Women*

My Aunt Miriam always says,
"The more the merrier,
unless you're talking about chins."

We don't have any eccentrics in our family, except for Aunt Bessie. She collects gravel.

My cousin Gladys was never interested in guys. But you know, she's very happy. And if you ever need your radiator flushed, she's your man.

Aunt Frieda—all she ever wanted to be was a Rockette. She made the height requirement. It was the width that was the problem.

My Aunt Pola went into the hospital for bursitis. She got a bedsore, which turned into phlebitis, which caused a stroke . . . although, if they ever settle, she'll be the richest vegetable in Bay Shore.

I really owe my sister Nadine.
We came out of the same womb.
Only she weighed thirteen pounds.
After her, Ma was a waterslide.
Why do you think I have
such a beautiful forehead?

I had to be a bridesmaid for my second cousin—once removed. And believe me, she was removed for a reason.

Gracie, when she's playing with my makeup, looks like my Aunt Shirley before her cataract surgery.

You don't know what torture is. My sister played the zither. One time my ears actually bled.

My sister, the caterer, works every holiday. Thank God we fast on Yom Kippur, or we'd never see her.

My Aunt Ida looks a lot
like Gene Shalit. I told her,
if she's going to dye her hair,
she should do the mustache too.

My Aunt Selma lives in Philadelphia.
She's the one with the miracle ear.
If you look in, you can see the
Virgin Mary. She can't have her ears
pierced—they keep healing.

Then there was my late great-aunt Mimma Fayga. I remember in the winter she used to wrap me up in this coat with her, my head right under her bosoms. My ears never got cold. I looked like Princess Leia. Until Mimma got old, then I looked like Goofy.

The Nanny on Ma

Far be it from me to rain on anyone's parade. That's my mother's job.

Ma doesn't like taking chances. This is a woman whose idea of a risk is wearing white pants to Tony Roma's.

My mother says she's fifty.
Think it's the truth?
Please, the only thing more stretched
are Clinton's bicycle shorts.
Fifty billion served and
that's just the White House.

You should have seen Ma's old nose.
She could hook a marlin.

Ma has plastic on the furniture. She's preserving it for the afterlife.

My mother makes a blintz that could double for a bedspread.

Ma's always reminding me that she was in labor with me for ten hours on account of my big head. I've told her it will never happen again.

My mother was stuffing herself with
pastrami right up until my birth.
I'm surprised I wasn't born
with a pickle in my mouth.

Fourteen is a very vulnerable age. I remember once my mother picked me up from school in a halter top and pedal pushers. I'm still looking for the right support group.

I swore I'd never be like my mother.
But I still have to fight the urge to
wash out gefilte fish jars
and use them for glasses.

My parents were on "Let's Make a Deal." Nine hundred people knew it was door number one. But they had to have the box. P.S., Carol Merrill on a giant tricycle. If my mother hadn't had an egg timer in her purse, we woulda come home with bubkes.

In my house, if we didn't talk about the dead, we'd have nothing to talk about except food. That's the great thing about funerals, you get both.

THE CHANUKAH BUSH

One year we begged my mother for a Christmas tree from Woolworth's. She called it a Chanukah bush. P.S., the candles from the menorah set the flocking on fire, and the fumes put my father in the emergency room. Meanwhile, my mother took this as a sign from God, and from then on we spent every Christmas at the Fontainbleu in Miami. To this day, I can't get a whiff of Bain de Soleil without having a yen for eggnog.

The Nanny on
the British

I've often wondered how the British know what anyone's feeling. They all must wear mood rings.

It's a small world. Niles spent his summers at Stratford-upon-Avon. I spent my summers selling Avon.

Niles told me that steak and kidney pie was Princess Diana's favorite. And they wonder why she throws up.

It's like when Mr. Sheffield's sister was going to marry this duke. I pointed out that we had never had a duke in the family. Then I remembered that we did, but we had to put him to sleep.